Petals of the Moon

A Poetry Collection

C. Churchill

Also, by C. Churchill:

Wildflower Tea

Color Body Feels

I am a Woman not a Winston

C. Churchill on social media:

Instagram @cc_writes

Facebook @cchurchillwrites

"All things are possible

Under the light of the moon."

Petals of the Moon

New

In the darkest of night

When toss and turn is all we know

When the sheep have lost

And the wolves have spoken

We drift lucid

Unafraid

Into the shadow of the moon

This is where we begin

under a new moon

I sat with the calm

The buzzing of new life

In my ear a torture

Reminding me

No matter how

No matter when

I cannot escape

The buzzing

The chaos

Distant memories rush

To the surface

After the day's tidings are sung a lullaby

And I still

Hoping my breath doesn't catch

On the images of you

in the still

C. Churchill

Midnight smells of

Sickly smoke

And wilted roses

I have yet to see otherwise

scent of you

The blades spin relentless

Above

Singing to me

The song of summer winds

With the click of repetition

Around and round we go

The tick of the clock

The click of the fan

The ceiling that has been swallowed

In night yet again

Void a star to see

But these eyes search wildly

Looking past shadows

Looking into further

Looking until my eyes burn, and tears fall

And night has won an audience

audience of one

I flirted with the darkness one night

Lit the puff of a cigarette

Behind the barn

Before double digits

Far too young to know of cancer

Far too young to care

I flirted with the darkness

Many nights in cemeteries

Playing with a high

Balanced between

Fear and papers

Sometimes rolled

Sometimes dipped

I flirted with the darkness

While bottles clinked

Among naked limbs

And disheveled clothes

The floor covered in madness

For a day nothing more

I flirted with the darkness

Eventually it noticed me

After many years of teasing

It took me as its own

It never promised the moon

Never promised the stars

Just took my hand

And led me to a place

I was no longer seen.

invisible

C. Churchill

When shadows turn

And demons churn

I see midnight strike again

In all its glory

A fit of pique

Filling night

Taunting sleep

Here I lay

Bound by fear

In silence

Under the cover of darkness

fear bound

The monsters under my bed

Hum lullabies

In the rhythm of my tears

Beautiful

Haunting

Lullabies

lullabies

C. Churchill

How do we walk

Where we can't find footing

How do we walk

Where we can't see

When the world disappears

Into the flatness of night

We are told to move forward

But this is not without fear

Never without fear

How do we walk

When we are

Paralyzed

As we step blindly

Into tombs of the unknown

Holding nothing but the flame of bravery

In shaking hands

We walk

We step forward

Hoping there is no wind

For this flame is unsure

Hoping the earth holds us dear

That gravity does not fail

That bravery is here.

We step forward

Hoping

That the abyss catches us

Just so.

bravery

C. Churchill

Sometimes the night

Gives me what I seek

As I lay

My body starts to calm

The void wraps around me

Like a hug from a year gone

The memory of you

Closing in

As my heart drifts to a calm melody

And all I can think

Is welcome back

I have been waiting for you

welcome

I often wonder

As my mind seizes in the hours between

When the sandman runs over pillows

And tracks dreams over closed eyes

If he sees me stirring

In my uncomfortable wait

His fingers poised and ready

To drop a sprinkling of peace

Over these eyes

Over these dreams

I wonder

Does he see me

Bartering my life

Trading memories

For a moment of peace each night

barter

C. Churchill

I called to the night

Awaiting answers

Beyond taillights

Before dawn

In the expanse

I stilled

As sunless chills

Crept faithfully in

I called to the night

Awaiting answers

My spine began to ache in the darkness

A full embrace

Wrapping my shoulders

To my ribs

Slowing a heart in beats

Meant for death

I called to the night

Awaiting answers

Just as my body became numb to light

Hope began to flicker

Faint to sight

Over my weary eyes

Spread thin

A shadow dances

Under soft wrought pain

Losing hope and back again

The waiting was over

I hit the bottom

My voice echoes

As answers come from within

Washing over me

Begging

Asking for this dance

Awaiting my answer

night dance

C. Churchill

Phantom memories of my past

Fade in and out

Like stars on a cloudy night

The harder I try to see

The more I lose sight

Without direction

I wander

Without the moon

I am lost

lost

Shackless of day pressed into oblivion

The verse held so tightly

In my thoughts

No room to spare

Unrequited love forcing this hand

To let go

Bleeding through pages

As hours turn to eternity

The darkest tales

My soul can no longer keep

For night is an ocean

And these thoughts

Have no longer the will

To swim

drown

C. Churchill

If you could only taste my fear

How deep it runs for you

But my demons taste like peppermints

And they are always offering.

candy

I lay under this blanket of night

The stars no longer seek

For I have turned my eyes

Towards the vanity of my deep

Searching an answer

In loves cruel game

An answer of less than my worthy name

For I have sold and bought this soul

Many times, over for those in the know

Where else can I seek?

When the night lasts eternity

And my eyes are begging

To simply believe

believe

Toss

Turn

Flip the spoon

I hear your heart

But I cannot feel it

Arms are empty of everything

But spite

Toss

Turn

Flip the spoon

Other side of the pillow

Maybe the chill will match the tone

Maybe we can ignore these hearts

Of stone

Toss

Turn

Flip the spoon

Sleeping isn't coming

Another night laid in arms

That have forgotten their role

That have forgotten to hold

Toss

    Turn

        Drop the spoon

    Lay straight like a dinner service

    In an empty room

Toss

    Turn

        Wake

Repeat.

    Waiting for a meal

        From a left-over dinner plate.

spoon

C. Churchill

Wash me in the river

Scrub my heart clean

It has been dirtied in ways

You have never seen

But your hands can find me

I have faith in that

It is there

Where one heart reaches

Again, and back

dirty hearts

We said it was forever

We said it was fate

We claimed our flag

Our hearts were staked

We were impossible to beat

In this world less humanity

Until we saw

Our mirror cracked

In vanity

vanity

Have you ever tried to hold onto things in the night?

In total darkness

Reaching

Reaching out

After it slipped just for a second

A moment

You heard it fall

Knock against your foot

Roll a bit

Then gone

You crumble

Hands searching

On a floor you have walked a thousand times

Where did it go?

You just had it

Your hands relentless

On hard smooth ground

Far and wide

Till knees are crushed

Under a weight of guilt

Your tongue burns

In words that cannot be taken back

But your hands still grasp

In the first moments of dawn

All you find is bloodied knees

Empty hands

And words that fill the floor

hold your tongue

When I lay you down to sleep

I pray the night your love will keep

For darkness plagues

The minds that wander

And I watch your breath

Under a new moon squander

Looking for a timbre

To lead me home

In love sweet love

It is all unknown

For the reaper comes

At every glance

Telling my heart

It has no chance

unknown

I wish I could stop seeing you in the night

And start seeing me.

blinded by memory

C. Churchill

In the darkest hour

Birds still

 On branches

Resting for a song

Night hunters

Had their kill

Now sleep with bellies full

I was born just before dawn

In the darkest hour

While the world

Was asleep

No coos

 No cries

 Just silence

I learned to wake

While the birds are still

I learned to wake

While hunters are asleep from fill

I learned the loneliness that comes before dawn

Not a peep from the darkness

Just shadows lay upon shadows

No songs

No kill

Stark and barren

But the silence has a comfort

And the lonely as well

I often wonder why I still search for a reason behind this hell

And continue to sift through

The loneliness in the darkest hour

When all I have known Is silence

darkest hour

C. Churchill

I lost another night of sleep

As if I would sleep anyway

The dark season has been here awhile

I doubt the sun even recalls my name

Although my laughter

Is logged in memory

And the sun begs a smile daily

This will be a season I remember

When tears tattooed my pillow

And sleep forgot to come home

forgotten sleep

My demons curled tightly

Around my thirst

Begging to be quenched

In my tranquil desert

But the stars, oh the stars

They shined in rain

Shined so brightly

Upon this pain

Thirsty I was

Amidst the flood

Amidst the life

I lost in love

But still I sat

Among the pain

Among the stars

Among the rain

For I knew

My wishes may come true

If the stars could find the moon

Behind clouds of blue

clouds of blue

C. Churchill

I hate the nights

When I sit

Pondering

What was

What could have been

Searching a never-ending sky

As if it will tell me why

But I still do

I think we all do

Especially those nights

When the stars have sunken deep behind clouds

When the moon has left us only with tides

It won't come back

That life

The one we search for

The one the stars hide from

The one where our sky has turned to black

Where memories flood

Of a life that seemed complete

A life we were strangely now worthy of

Suddenly

When our canvas is blank?

And the world is as open as it can get

We still ponder

On what was

When the moon has hidden

Giving us the gift of

New

fresh start

C. Churchill

I bathe in the night

Hoping to wash the darkness

Back to the sky

That has given it to me

Scrub hard

Then harder

Trying to release my shadows

But they grasp tightly

To my core

And smile

Laughing at my dimwitted hands

That travel my darkness

Because I don't even know where to wash

I don't even know

Where or how far the darkness has gone

my darkness

It suffocates you know

The night

With a heaviness

Not just on my chest

But in my veins

Waiting for morning

Waiting to breathe again

heaviness

Crescent

C. Churchill

I have learned to see in the dark

I have learned to love my sadness

take the time

I walked away from the day

Held hands with the sky

Watched clouds dance with stars

No longer wondering why

I let it go

Let it all out

Tear soaked pillows

With a side of hope

starting to dream

C. Churchill

My spirit swallowed the shadows

Kissed death like lilies

On a summer breeze

I had no fear of the villain

I had no fear of the monster

I had no fear

At all

A strangeness arose

In my sublimity

While the shadows filled vacancies

Where friends used to dwell

Dark alleys were no longer pin drop quiet

But welcoming with the hum of possibility

I relished in the completeness

While memories faded into night

Death becomes

A grace we call upon

Drinking in darkness

Filling every hole

No void left unnamed

The shadow

The monster

An ally

To drink from

To eat from

To live

To become

Possibly the most feared

Villain of them all

fearless

C. Churchill

Last nail in the coffin

Last bridge to burn

Cut them all down

With a memory short term

In anguish

We see

What life was really meant to be

There are no fairy tales

On this side of the tracks

Knowing coffins aren't nailed

And burned bridges can't come back

Play that hand wisely

And you too shall see

It's all a game of chess

And you can be Queen

winning

They held me back

Like a lap dog

Feeding me scraps in tandem

Confused

Running in circles

As the bits fell to the ground

I couldn't find my way

So, I stayed

In circles

For scraps

To survive

But god dammit

I was still starving

Under the bravado of love

Until I became a cannibal

cannibal

C. Churchill

Fierce, oh no

Never fierce

Just sweetness

With a side of survival

survivor

I sat under the night

This time with

Fresh eyes

Not waiting

But wanting

A realization occurred

Between tried and true

Those who become wolf

Are only controlled by the moon

control

With a heart as black as death

His midnight lashes

Grazed me bare

I was slick

But not as he

I was thirsty, he was sin

And by god

I never let them in

But this stranger

A bottle service

Sent by the night

And relentless

For my taste

Just one sip

Just one little sip

Then he could go

But those lashes

Told a different story

One where I was no longer in control

When the table flips

And the tail spin begins

Oil and water

Fight to get in

A myriad of lust, power and fruition

Is no easy task when you are on a mission

But sometimes the task is worth the reward

In a kill or be killed world

killers

C. Churchill

Place those roses

On frozen ground

Be sure to wipe your feet

It's never as it seems in your dreams

Now is it?

We battle. We score

We soak in sorrows

Nevermore

But still we believe

In love you see

On travelers

Passing in the night

Biding time

When the feeling is right

No not them

They are place keepers

Peace keepers

Grooming us for the real thing

Saving our madness for shoes

By the door of tomorrow

doors of tomorrow

If I asked you to sleep with my demons

Would you say yes?

baggage always included

C. Churchill

Are we not wilted by the sun?

Are we not just visitors in this life?

Where we take refuge

We take our sorrow

And bury it in the night

Where flesh is ripped by teeth

And we bite for more

Because our pain is never full

Of the constant escape we seek

escape

A black cat crossed my path

While the umbrella spread open

I let him in

Under the ladder

Filling all my superstitions

On the 13th floor

The one just above

Happily, ever after

I made peace

With darkness

superstition

C. Churchill

I tend to watch the sky

Look for the changes

Where will Orion greet me tonight?

Will it be at my side

Or above?

Has the North Star decided?

If I am worthy

Or I am blind?

I tend to watch the sky

Look for the changes

Some nights I tire

Rest my head on bricks

Let my fingers trail

The empty bed space

Not searching, just feeling

I tend to watch the sky

Look for the changes

Observe all I know

All I have learned

And all I have lost

Seeking meaning in the now warm side of the bed

I tend to watch the sky

Look for the changes

As the universe shines down

With every answer

Behind the lips of the moon

And I contemplate

And I tire

Blowing a kiss till tomorrow

blowing a kiss

C. Churchill

I wrote the roses love songs

And watered them in grief

My heart lay under

Next to muddy shoes

Such a mess I made

For the roses that wilted

As soon as they touched my hands

 I wrote love songs

And sacrificed tears

But forgot my heart wasn't even there

underneath love

My darling

If you could only see

What wonder could be made

From a few pieces of torn heartstrings

And a locket on a broken chain

My darling

If you could only see

There is still love

In these remains

remains

C. Churchill

I have played the fiddle

The piper

The priest

I have seen the devil flown

A flock of geese

I have wearied a traveler

I have bedded a monk

I have been there and back

Stilled breath in lungs

Caused hearts to beat

Caused hearts to weep

Never lost but a night of sleep

For they say

Who buys the cow?

When the milk is free

But my debt isn't to you

Them or me.

It's to grief.

And I am not sure

That has a payback

For this heart

Lost all worth

When it hit the floor

And now is still

Trying to climb

Beyond closed doors

Lock and key

My tears hold strong

For a debt

I am trying to pay back

With a shitty love song

shitty love songs

C. Churchill

I am looking for a dreamer

One to hold my sin

Look at my pieces

Like they got a win

Instead I find paupers

Playing a fool's game

Scraping my love

Off someone else's name

I am looking for a dreamer

In a house of cards

Where one breath stolen

Could cause the fall

falling for you

If I greet you with a smile

Look at my eyes

They always tell the truth

the truth lies within

C. Churchill

I have been there naked

Starving

Waiting

For a bus that will never come

Watching the moon traverse the sky

From dusk till dawn

My feet have lost the urge to step further

And the bench is no longer warm

My thin bones beg for sleep

Chilled in the path of darkness

But I wait

For the moon crosses

In my sight

On heavy lids

A glow

A strange glow

Under this trance

Naked and starving

A high, in a low

Why mystery exists

And busses never come

And thoughts lay with the moon

But never the sun

I wait

For a bus that never existed

In a trance

Brought by the moon

That has never left

trance

C. Churchill

We all walk in pictures

Of what we want to portray

In a world where mistakes

Can ruin more than a day

Claiming ground

Where sacred has lost meaning

And truth has been shoved

 In the corner left bleeding

For who are you?

Is it for them?

Have you told your truth

To stop begging again

Lashed it with lies

Told it everything is fine

A smile

A filter

All in a day's work

Walking in pictures

Away from the truth

filters

I was chained to the day

Suffocating

In a collar thicker than the skin it rested upon

Twisted nonbelievers

Told me I could never win

I could never free

Never begin

Branded in this life

In his death

In a senseless act of violence

Left widow

And nonsense

Try as I did

I no longer fit in

Widowed in name, in place, in friend

I left the day

Left it for them

And took my place in the night

Where collars were for lips

And chains were nonexistent

night calling

C. Churchill

Run with me

Naked

Under June skies

As they release

Rain a flood

Run with me

Naked

Feel the clouds

Free themselves

We will lay the same

On fields of pleasure

Their release wetting ours

Lay with me

Flesh upon flesh

Trickle down into shadows

Filling our darkness

Awakening a pulse

That had forgotten its pace

Lay with me

As the sky washes us free

From parched hearts

From parched voids

From a thirst

Stay with me

Naked

Free

In all things that are real

Let the June sky

Release a flood

In lieu of flowers

in lieu of flowers

C. Churchill

Let's kiss our way

Beyond the stars

And spend time

Exploring the universe

The clocks will shift

As they always do

For those who

Drink of the moon

And swallow

Forever

kiss me

One day I felt the earth tremble

One day it did quake

It tore love from my arms

In a true force way

There is no revenge

There is no plotting

For how we can battle the universe deciding

So, we plant our feet and extend our reach

Hoping the universe hears our plea

screaming

C. Churchill

I walk along the road

Wave to the passerby

Smiling

With unsteady eyes

A common occurrence

Yes, I know

But awkward now in my timbers

Those smiles for no one

How obligatory

I have become

Blaming it on awkward

A staple left hanging

From another time

Just far enough away

To not cause damage

The faded paint peels

On this empty house

And the only ones who see

Smile

And wave

Fallen photographs collect dust

On a floor

Letting them know

We don't live here anymore

For in everyday life

There are many small deaths

Brought on by the obligations

Of awkwardness

small deaths

C. Churchill

My darkness is growing lighter

With every bridge I burn

open skies

The night has my throat

A death tight grip

Begging submission

In every slip

My torture

My tears

My tender misgivings

I am learning to trust the hands of darkness

And trying to breathe

While suffocating

Who will win?

trust

Full

C. Churchill

I remember

The night I met the moon

There were a million stars

And silky layers of fireflies

The grass was cool under my feet

I remember

The night the moon met me

I was crumpled in tears

There were no fireflies

Nor silky layers

There was grass under my feet

And not much else

Through blinding waves of tears and darkness

The moon said stay

And I remain

no matter what

Let me wander

Let me free

Let me out from the things we see

Into the night please let me go

Untie my hands from what I know

Where I am

Where I am supposed to be

It is all too much

For one soul to bear

When the world looks sideways

And forgets you are right there

unseen

C. Churchill

I don't know time

Like I once did

Its been winter for more than a song

The nights long

The birds sleeping

Blankets of white

Echo spaces

But I cannot say if it is midnight yet

Or even Tuesday night

I don't know time

Like I once did

Thoughts are frozen

Stilled

On the banks of forever

Losing change

Like holed pockets

From hands just trying to find warmth

I don't know time

Like I once did

Scrolling

Instead of strolling

The moon phases

Phase

The arms of every clock

Blur in a daze

I don't know time

Like I once did

But I know my arms miss the minutes

And I know my hands miss the warmth

And I know

I miss you

always

Ravens stretched

Across my breath

Feathers longing to get in

They want this flight

More than I

But I am finally

Ready to give in

it's time

The sun warmed my heart

But the moon warmed my soul

moonchild

C. Churchill

If I sit

For hours

Take me

Take me to the night

Show me

The birds that sing

Under shadows

Show me the moon glow

Across webs we don't see during the day

Show me

A magic I cannot see

During the bustle of normalcy

For the day holds tight

And I cannot see past circumstance

Where wee hours have held little charm

I am now ready

To experience

Darkness

fully

When stars align

And beauty has no price

I wish my hand in yours

We have fought clouds of fury

Under the weight of backbones

Bending

Twisting

To comply

Lashed by the sun

In all the wrong ways

Driven into the night

This passion plays

Not for the weak

Not for the weary

But reserved for those

Who seek true beauty

true beauty

His hands

Had no quiver

Steady as the horizon

Over curves of heartache

They traveled

But my body could not compete

Earth quakes

Earth shakes

Memories of unsteady hands and wavering glances

Plagued me

I had wanton eyes before

As well as wanton hands

But I have never had these hands

These eyes

Steady

Assured

Knowing a place

Knowing a future

The universe had spoken

Placed a pulse in my path

One to hold my nights

One to hold my gaze

But I could not look

I could not see

I was ritual

He was free

And I spoke in terms

While he spoke in energy

Two fish out of water

Searching for common air

I wonder if we can

Ever learn to breathe

learning

C. Churchill

We are all monsters

We are all saints

Maybe that is everyone's fate.

nonexclusive

I have been calloused

Beyond a labor life

Hardened beyond acceptable

My walls a labyrinth

No seeker has yet found

I wait in the center of this maze

On a throne with no name

Ruling the sky of little place

The smaller it gets

The less I know

I still rule

That is the only way to go

I support these walls

This kingdom

Of no one

stubborn

The trees have been bent

In a heart shaped vise

Someone has stolen their sun

For the love of the moon

For the love of the night

Who is to say they will not grow?

For now, they form a beautiful

Whole

whole

When sleep doesn't come

I hear your name

I have pushed you back to the recess

You don't arrive on time

You never did

Only when I am bleeding want

From my eyes

From my soul

Only then you arrive

a text or two later

C. Churchill

I thought I lost my purpose

I thought I lost my way

I gave a dollar change

For a penny play

Breaking up windows

Slamming doors

I forgot my purpose

Wasn't their way

I gave rage and heartache

A brand-new face

When I lost every bit

Of assumed grace

On that dark day

When the clouds came home

They expected a widow forlorn

When they assumed my fire would die

I slammed the door but did not cry

For this fire within won't let me lie

Won't let me sit

Won't let me stay

It won't let me be less than I was

Before that day

The day you left

Dropping breath away

In that moment

I found my way

There is no map for the unseen

Just our fire within

And our will to breathe

I still have mine

It is not gone

It never left

Well at least for long

This heart still beats

And it still loves

With all the passion

Right where it belongs

Strong

On fire

And very much alive

hearts of fire

C. Churchill

Gangrene

Of the heart

Where honey once flowed

Is a sickness we all know

Where it no longer pumps the way, it did

When I love you

Was fluid and filled to the brim

Overflowing chaos

Sticky and sweet

Where the sky was only ours to meet

A love where two is the only view

That love

The one you know is true

When that love is gone

We shrivel

In sickness. In darkness

As if we have lost a limb

As if we didn't know

Love is a war

And there are always casualties

gangrene of the heart

I have slept with the moon all my life

What makes you think you can take its place

Yes, I adore you

This is true

But will you be like the moon

Will you stay?

night after night

I couldn't stop you

Just as I couldn't stop the sun

Nor the moon

But I always wished

You would have stopped me

from running

I remember when I feared the night

Feared the sea

The open

Abyss

Where thoughts get lost

And then some found

Looking further than a shore

Further than a nightlight

That I had in my youth

The one that kept the monsters away

Looking into something I have never had to focus on

It crippled me

Shot arrows through my faith

As I bled out on every shore

The moon shone a light

More beautiful than any sunrise

More beautiful than the known

I suppose that is when I found

The night was my home

home

C. Churchill

I held it

In my pocket

Like a wish

I tried not to crush it

And keep it safe

I really did

I placed it gently

As if it were my only gift

I tried not to disturb it

No compromise

No jostling

Just letting it be

But when the rains came

And night had its way

My hands were not enough

To keep it from stray

For I have never held gold

Nor diamonds of treasure

Only things that dulled in time

I could not stop the storm

The wind

Nor the rain

And my pockets seemed flooded

Yet again

I still lay in puddles of regret

Where my hands should have been

What treasures I could have held

If only these hands were capable

capable

C. Churchill

When my world falls apart

I bare my shoulders

And walk straight into darkness

For my soul knows its place

And in the sun, I only burn

Chaos is for the plenty

And I am well preserved

immortal

Happiness was stolen

Like a babe in the night

Leaving a hollow

And I still look to the moon

For why

questions

C. Churchill

Lay me down in fields of plenty

Watch me writhe

For I have no expectations when it comes to thighs

And what's laid between them

And what produces lies

For I have seen the magic

On a stage show

Not meant for me

Might as well put mirrors in all the rooms

So, they can see the girth

Of rise

Laid heavy to bed

While my heart cringes in corners of

A fairytale life

Where intimate means

Love

And naked means birth

But yes, my friend

Give me your hollow girth

Full of less expectations

Than church on Sunday

Full of sinners

At His behest

A few sins from a blessing

But always once removed

Trojan warrior please

Give it your all

Because my sad self

Has realized

This life

Is full of expecting

And no one living up to it

hollow girth

C. Churchill

I walk the line

Of sanity and the other

Knowing what is real

But never really accepting it

The more I see the pain

In my everyday

The more I retreat

Saving myself

For better days

Some say wise

Some say the other

I don't know what to say

Amidst my minds sweet stutter

stutter

I went out into the darkness

I yelled

Not at you

Not for you

But for me

For my lungs

To shake

For my ears

To hear

For my heart

To skip a beat

I went out into the darkness

To remember

That I was not

Obsolete

alive

C. Churchill

You can only toss and turn so much

Before the pillow knows you well

Knows all your secrets

All your tears

Your frustrations

Your fears

You can only toss and turn so much

Before the moon has your number

And you wander

From what you know

Leaving behind

Pillows soaked in regret

Pulling up your finest

Packaging it

Not in hope

Not in desperation

But in a beginning

Take it from me

It's never too late

To start fresh

Take all those ideas

You had about life

And throw them

Out the nearest window

And while you are at it

Look out

Look up

Look at this expanse

Once you are done with the pillows

Once you are done tossing and turning

You will see

This world misses you

This sky misses you

And it is there for you

Always

When you are ready

ready for life

C. Churchill

I sat on the edge of longing

Just long enough

To see

My reflection still

My dreams dissipate

And my hope drown

Breath was shallow

And my image clear

All I can say to the waters

So faithfully drowning me was

Thank you for holding me just under life

And as tricky as it was to find footing

I became a better swimmer

Than you ever expected

better than expected

We leave bread crumbs in the sky

And call them constellations

Building galaxies

Far and wide

Hoping

They will lead us home

But all we know for certain

In a full sky

Is something

Has changed

And this address

Travels

Because home

Travels

As sure as footing becomes lost

And our hearts do the same

The moon will still phase

The tides will always come

And energy will always stir us

To our every bone

Making magic is possible

And full moons worthy

We continue

We will be making a new sky

In every step we take

And the only magic we need to worry about

Is moving forward

Because of all the breadcrumbs I have left

I can look up any night

And see that I am still

Traveling

And finding home

traveler

It was never about the moon

It was about me finally seeing it.

awake

"The moon has saved me

More times than I can count."

This collection is dedicated to those who have spent a night or longer sleepless and troubled.

You are not alone.

Poems and pages

C. Churchill

About the Author

Churchill enjoys a quiet life creating art and writing. She spends her days enjoying the natural beauty of her Michigan home. After the death of her father when she was a child, she became an avid reader. Her love of books led her to start writing. After the murder of her husband in 2006 she pursued a Bachelors in Theatre and followed with a Master's in Education. She enjoys teaching visual art and writing to young adults and helping them find their voice.

Books by C. Churchill

Wildflower Tea

Color Body Feels

I am a Woman not a Winston

C. Churchill on social media

Instagram @cc_writes

Facebook @cchurchillwrites

Made in the USA
San Bernardino, CA
01 July 2020

74632638R00069